A Note From Rick Renner

I am on a personal quest to see a "revival of the Bible" so people can establish their lives on a firm foundation that will stand strong and endure the test as end-time storm winds begin to intensify.

In order to experience a revival of the Bible in your personal life, it is important to take time each day to read, receive, and apply its truths to your life. James tells us that if we will continue in the perfect law of liberty — refusing to be forgetful hearers, but determined to be doers — we will be blessed in our ways. As you watch or listen to the programs in this series and work through this corresponding study guide, I trust you will search the Scriptures and allow the Holy Spirit to help you hear something new from God's Word that applies specifically to your life. I encourage you to be a doer of the Word He reveals to you. Whatever the cost, I assure you — it will be worth it.

> Thy words were found, and I did eat them;
> and thy word was unto me the joy and rejoicing of mine heart:
> for I am called by thy name, O Lord God of hosts.
> —Jeremiah 15:16

Your brother and friend in Jesus Christ,

Rick Renner

Transformed
Personal Encounters With God

Published by Rick Renner Ministries
www.renner.org

ISBN 13: 978-1-6675-0411-7

eBook ISBN 13: 978-1-6675-0412-4

How To Use This Study Guide

This five-lesson study guide corresponds to *"Transformed" With Denise Renner* **(Renner TV)**. Each lesson in this study guide covers a topic that is addressed during the program series, with questions and references supplied to draw you deeper into your own private study of the Scriptures on this subject.

To derive the most benefit from this study guide, consider the following:

First, watch or listen to the program prior to working through the corresponding lesson in this guide. (Programs can also be viewed at **renner.org** by clicking on the Media/Archives links or on our Renner Ministries YouTube channel.)

Second, take the time to look up the scriptures included in each lesson. Prayerfully consider their application to your own life.

Third, use a journal or notebook to make note of your answers to each lesson's Study Questions and Practical Application challenges.

Fourth, invest specific time in prayer and in the Word of God to consult with the Holy Spirit. Write down the scriptures or insights He reveals to you.

Finally, take action! Whatever the Lord tells you to do according to His Word, do it.

For added insights on this subject, it is recommended that you obtain Denise Renner's book ***Unstoppable: Pressing Through Fear, Offense, and Negative Opinions To Fulfill God's Purpose***. You may also select from Rick and Denise's available resources by placing your order at **renner.org** or by calling 1-800-742-5593.

TOPIC

Hagar — From Runaway Slave to Mother of Many

SYNOPSIS

The five lessons in this study titled *Transformed* will focus on the following individuals:

- Hagar — From Runaway Slave to Mother of Many
- Elijah — From Depression to Resurrection
- Jacob — From Deceiver to Prince With God
- Gideon — From Hidden to Hero
- Nebuchadnezzar — From Arrogant King to Worshiper of God

When we come to Jesus — or Jesus comes to us — and He touches us, change is going to take place. There's just no way our lives will remain the same when we saturate ourselves in God's Word and seek His presence. We see this dynamic on display in the lives of people in both the Old and New Testaments — including the life of Hagar, Abraham and Sarah's (formerly named Abram and Sarai) Egyptian slave girl.

The emphasis of this lesson:

Hagar, the maidservant of Sarai, was misused and treated harshly by Sarai, so Hagar ran away from her. The Lord Himself went looking for Hagar and found her. He promised her she would give birth to a son and that He would multiply her descendants exceedingly. The encounter she experienced with the Lord transformed her life.

We Are Transformed From Glory to Glory

Before we look at the example of Hagar, let's talk for a moment about transformation. In Second Corinthians 3:18, the apostle Paul said, "But we all, with unveiled face, beholding as in a mirror the glory of the Lord, are being transformed into the same image from glory to glory, just as by the Spirit of the Lord."

The "mirror" referred to here is the Word of God. James, the half-brother of Jesus, also described the Bible as a mirror, telling us that "…he who looks into the perfect law of liberty and continues in it, and is not a forgetful hearer but a doer of the work, this one will be blessed in what he does" (James 1:25). When we "behold" truth in God's Word and fill our mind and heart with it, we are looking at the image of Jesus, and as we look at His image, we become like what we see. In other words, we share in Jesus' glory!

This amazing transformation also takes place when we spend time with Jesus — praying and sitting still in His presence. Investing time focusing on Christ is so powerful. The Bible says, "Those who look to him are radiant…" (Psalm 34:5 *ESV*). Think about it. The moment we repent of our sin and invite Christ into our life, we're saved, and the very Spirit of God comes to live inside us (*see* Galatians 4:6). Friend, you can't be with God and walk away the same. Transformation is bound to take place.

Hagar Was Misused and Treated Harshly by Sarai

When most people think about the transforming power of God, they don't usually think of Hagar, but she, too, is an example of what happens when one receives and believes God's Word. Hagar was Sarai's Egyptian maidservant who was likely acquired during Abraham's stay in Egypt when a great famine struck the region.

The Bible tells us that Sarai was unable to have a child, and after decades of struggling to conceive, Sarai decided to do what was a customary practice among many barren women: She gave her servant girl (Hagar) to her husband in hopes that the servant would conceive a child. If she did conceive, by law, that child could be claimed by Sarai as her own. Genesis 16:2-4 says:

> **So Sarai said to Abram, "See now, the Lord has restrained me from bearing children. Please, go in to my maid; perhaps I shall obtain children by her." And Abram heeded the voice of Sarai. Then Sarai, Abram's wife, took Hagar her maid, the Egyptian, and gave her to her husband Abram to be his wife, after Abram had dwelt ten years in the land of Canaan. So he went in to Hagar, and she conceived. And when she saw that she had conceived, her mistress became despised in her eyes.**

Interestingly, once Hagar became pregnant, she began to have an attitude with Sarai, who had authority over her. God predicted this type of response in Proverbs 30:23 where He talks about two of the four things that the earth cannot bear. The verse identifies these things as, "A hateful woman when she is married, and a maidservant who succeeds [supplants or usurps] her mistress." That's what Hagar did — she successfully conceived a child, which her mistress had been unable to do, and as a result, Hagar saw herself as better than Sarai. Indeed, this was a terribly unbearable situation to navigate.

Scripture says, "Then Sarai said to Abram, 'My wrong be upon you! I gave my maid into your embrace; and when she saw that she had conceived, I became despised in her eyes. The Lord judge between you and me'" (Genesis 16:5). Here, it's as if Sarai is saying, "I don't know whose fault it is that we're dealing with this servant who has a heart of hatred toward me, so may the Lord judge who is in the wrong."

Verse 6 says, "…Abram said to Sarai, 'Indeed your maid is in your hand; do to her as you please.' And when Sarai dealt harshly with her, she fled from her presence." In the midst of this terrible situation, Sarai becomes so angry and vengeful toward Hagar that she began to treat her harshly. One biblical commentator says that Sarai put extra work on her. Was Sarai trying to jeopardize Hagar's health? Was she trying to wear her down so she would lose the baby? Exactly what Sarai did we don't know. Scripture simply says that she dealt with Hagar harshly — so harshly that she ran away from Sarai.

God Always Comes Looking for Us

It's vital to note that nothing catches God by surprise. In His omniscience, He knew exactly how this surrogate-mother scenario was going to play out — including Sarai's harsh retaliation against Hagar for her servant's attitude toward her. Genesis 16:7 says, "Now the Angel of the Lord found her by a spring of water in the wilderness, by the spring on the way to Shur."

Many scholars believe that when the Angel of the Lord appeared to someone in the Old Testament it was a preincarnate appearance of Jesus, which is called a *Christophany*. Looking at the context of this verse, it certainly seems that the person who appeared to Hagar was the Lord Himself. No doubt, God has wanted to restore relationship with mankind since Adam and Eve's fall in the Garden of Eden, and His recurring appearances throughout the Old Testament confirm this desire.

In Genesis 16, we see Hagar has run away from the severe mistreatment of her mistress, Sarai. Likely exhausted from being afflicted by Sarai, Hagar took a moment to catch her breath and be refreshed by the spring of water in the wilderness. Question after question no doubt raced through her mind. *What am I going to do now? How am I going to feed and raise this child? What happens if someone finds me and discovers I'm a runaway slave?* As concern after concern swirled within Hagar, suddenly, "…The Angel of the Lord *found her*…" (*see* Genesis 16:7).

Did you know that a very similar situation happened to a blind man that Jesus healed? When the Pharisees learned that this man had been healed on the Sabbath, they threw him out of the synagogue. It was in that time of rejection and mistreatment that Jesus went and "found him" (John 9:35). Although the blind man wasn't looking for Jesus, Jesus was looking for him and found him. In addition to having his sight restored, he also was given the opportunity to put his faith in Jesus!

When Hagar was treated harshly by Sarai and ran away, God looked for her and found her. Likewise, when you've been hurt and rejected, God comes looking for you. He's your answer! He is the One who brings healing, strength, and restoration. And He provides the direction you need right when you need it. You might not be looking for God, but He is looking for you.

God Sees Our Affliction and Hears Our Cry

What happened when the Angel of the Lord found Hagar? The Bible says, "And He said, 'Hagar, Sarai's maid, where have you come from, and where are you going?' She said, 'I am fleeing from the presence of my mistress Sarai.' The Angel of the Lord said to her, 'Return to your mistress, and submit yourself under her hand'" (Genesis 16:8,9).

Can you imagine hearing those words? Hagar had run for her very life to escape Sarai's treatment of her, and now God was directing her to go back and surrender to Sarai again. However, God's direction came with a powerful promise:

…The Angel of the Lord said to her, "I will multiply your descendants exceedingly, so that they shall not be counted for multitude."

— **Genesis 16:10**

So the blessing of obeying God and returning to Sarai was that Hagar would not only have the baby she was carrying, but also a countless number of other descendants. The next verse says:

And the Angel of the Lord said to her: "Behold, you are with child, and you shall bear a son. You shall call his name Ishmael, because the Lord has heard your affliction."

— **Genesis 16:11**

Here we see that God had an impromptu gender reveal. "You're having a boy!" He announced, which was no doubt music to Hagar's ears. Then the Lord gave her the child's name — *Ishmael*, which means *the Lord hears*. Isn't it interesting that the verse doesn't say, "The Lord has heard Abraham's prayer"? Or, "The Lord has heard Sarai's complaining and has seen her anger"? No, it says, "…The Lord has heard *your* affliction" (Genesis 16:11).

Friend, your affliction has a sound. God hears when your heart is breaking. When something has been done to you or to someone you love — or you're in an overwhelming situation and don't know how you're going to get out of it — your affliction has a distinct sound that is heard by God. Wow!

Just imagine the pain that was filling Hagar's heart and the confusion that was bombarding her mind. *Sarai told me to sleep with Abraham,* she must have thought, *And he willingly had relations with me. When I conceived this baby Sarai asked for, she began beating and abusing me. Why? I did exactly what she asked me to do.* In the midst of Hagar's confusion, rejection, and pain, God heard her affliction, and He hears the affliction you're going through right now!

Hagar Had Seen God and Lived To Tell About It

The Angel of the Lord went on to tell Hagar that her son Ishmael would be "a wild man" and said, "…His hand shall be against every man, and every man's hand against him. And he shall dwell in the presence of all his brethren" (Genesis 16:12).

How did Hagar respond to what God said? Genesis 16:13 says:

> **Then she called the name of the Lord who spoke to her, You-Are-the-God-Who-Sees; for she said, "Have I also here seen Him who sees me?"**

This reaction from Hagar reveals that she was powerfully moved by what she heard, and the fact that she called the One who spoke to her "the God Who Sees" tells us clearly that the person who appeared to her was not just an angel. You wouldn't say to an angel, "You are the God Who Sees."

Interestingly, the words "seen Him" in Genesis 16:13 mean *seen the back of*. Do you remember when God revealed Himself to Moses when he was in the cleft of the rock? We read about it in Exodus 33:21-23. Moses couldn't look at the face of God, so God tucked him away in the cleft of the rock and allowed Moses to only see His back. Now we can understand why God would reveal Himself to Moses, but it's harder to understand why He would reveal Himself to an Egyptian slave girl who had been rejected.

Indeed, when God revealed Himself to Hagar, it was an encounter that transformed her life. Genesis 16:14 says, "Therefore the well was called Beer Lahai Roi…," which in Hebrew literally means *well of the One Who Lives and Sees Me* or, *Do I live after seeing God?* This Egyptian maidservant had seen God — and lived. That's exactly what happened to Jacob, which we will see in Lesson 3.

Again, when the comforting and affirming power of God touches your life, you are transformed. None of us can do enough or be good enough to receive His life-changing touch, and Hagar's life verifies this truth. Not even her status as an Egyptian slave girl could prevent God from finding her and comforting her with His presence.

Hagar ran away from Sarai rejected, confused, and not knowing if the baby she was carrying would live. But after her encounter with God, she received and obeyed His word, returning to Sarai with confidence because she knew she was going deliver a son and that countless other descendants would follow. Her life was transformed because of the presence of the Lord. That's powerful!

Denise Renner — Before and After God's Touch

In the program, Denise shared this testimony of how the presence of God touched her life many years ago:

In 1972, my life was transformed. I began hearing the Word of God and learning that I could be filled with the Holy Spirit. Although I didn't know what that meant, I continued to listen to the preaching of God's Word. I remember going to one particular meeting in which I came under such conviction that I couldn't hear anything that was said that night.

I went outside and sat on the street curb by myself. In that moment, I was just a powerless religious girl who was living in rebellion to my parents. Broken inside, I surrendered my heart to God, and His presence met me in an extraordinary way. Instantly, He transformed me into a new creation (*see* 2 Corinthians 5:17). I went home and apologized to my mother and quit rebelling against her. I also started boldly witnessing to people about Jesus.

Before that encounter with God, I was very insecure and scared to do anything for the Lord. But after He touched me, the fear was gone, and I was filled with His power. I even started my own hospital-visitation ministry. My life is a living example of God's transforming power!

Friend, you can't be touched by God and remain the same. His transforming power is still at work today! It's the very resurrection power of God that's working inside you right now.

This power transforms us day by day, from one degree of glory to another. Every time we meditate on His Word or spend time in His presence — praying, worshiping, and being still — we're changing and becoming more and more like Him.

STUDY QUESTIONS

> **Study to shew thyself approved unto God, a workman that needeth not to be ashamed, rightly dividing the word of truth.**
> **— 2 Timothy 2:15**

1. One of the greatest ways we are transformed is by spending time reading, studying, and meditating on God's Word. What are some of the scriptures the Holy Spirit has really made alive to you in your walk with Him? Take a few moments to write them down and share how they have transformed your life.

2. Just as Hagar's affliction was heard by God, your affliction reaches
    His ears too. When your heart is breaking, He is aware of it. What do
    Psalm 34:17-20 and Psalm 145:18 and 19 say about God's attentive-
    ness to your prayers?

PRACTICAL APPLICATION

**But be ye doers of the word, and not hearers only,
deceiving your own selves.
—James 1:22**

1. When God appeared to Hagar, He comforted her and gave her words
    of hope and direction. Can you remember a difficult time when you
    ran away or retreated in isolation because you were hurt or rejected?
    How did God meet you? Take a few moments to describe what was
    going on in your life and how the Lord comforted you with His
    presence.

2. Although none of us likes times of trials and troubles, they are often
    the times we draw closest to God. How has God used times of
    hardship and pain to reveal Himself to you and build His relationship
    with you?

TOPIC

Elijah — From Depression to Resurrection

SYNOPSIS

Of all the Old Testament prophets, Elijah stands out as having one of the
most dramatic ministries of all. He served during the reign of King Ahab
and Ahab's notorious wife, Jezebel, but Elijah is probably best remembered
for his faceoff with 450 prophets of Baal on Mount Carmel. Moreover,
Elijah is the same prophet who appeared with Moses and talked with
Jesus on the Mount of Transfiguration and is expected to return to earth
as one of the two Tribulation witnesses (*see* Revelation 11). In this lesson,

we'll focus on one snapshot from his life and see how he escaped the snare of depression and experienced a resurrection.

The emphasis of this lesson:

Elijah was a prophet used mightily by God to stomp out the worship of false gods during King Ahab's reign. After flowing powerfully in God's anointing, Elijah became physically, mentally, and emotionally exhausted, and fear entered his soul. Rather than judge Elijah, the Lord comforted him with much-needed food and rest, infusing him with strength and boldness to carry out his assignment.

God's Word and Presence Are Transforming!

Our anchor verse for this series is Second Corinthians 3:18, which says, "But we all, with unveiled face, beholding as in a mirror the glory of the Lord, are being transformed into the same image from glory to glory, just as by the Spirit of the Lord."

The moment you invite Jesus to be your Lord and Savior, a divine deposit of God's Spirit is placed inside you, and transformation begins. The Holy Spirit is the down payment of our spiritual inheritance in Christ (*see* Ephesians 1:13,14). He's also the supernatural agent of change that transforms our soul into the likeness of Jesus. When we get into God's Word, worship Him sincerely from our heart, or spend time with Him in prayer, something amazing takes place.

According to Second Corinthians 3:18, what we behold, we become. As we fix our eyes on Jesus, we are transformed into His glorious image in ever-increasing degrees. It's inevitable. When God's presence and power touch our life, we are never the same again.

Elijah Showcased God's Power on Mount Carmel

If anyone in the Old Testament was familiar with God's power, it was the prophet Elijah. His ministry began about 55 years after Solomon's death, and he served as God's mouthpiece to both the kingdom of Israel and Judah during a rebellious era. The most memorable display of God's power through Elijah took place during the reign of Ahab, king of Israel.

Jezebel, Ahab's wicked wife, had established idolatry and the worship of Baal throughout the land. To provoke the people to make a choice between God and Baal, Elijah told Ahab, "'Now therefore, send and gather all Israel to me on Mount Carmel, the four hundred and fifty prophets of Baal, and the four hundred prophets of Asherah, who eat at Jezebel's table.'" (1 Kings 18:19). Verses 19 and 20 continue, "So Ahab sent for all the children of Israel, and gathered the prophets together on Mount Carmel. And Elijah came to all the people, and said, 'How long will you falter between two opinions? If the Lord is God, follow Him; but if Baal, follow him.' But the people answered him not a word."

As you continue reading First Kings 18, you'll discover that there was a showdown between the prophets of Baal and Jehovah — the One True God. Two altars were set up with a sacrifice ready to be offered on each, and by the declaration of Elijah, "…the God who answers by fire, He is God" (1 Kings 18:24). Scripture says the prophets of Baal cried out from morning till afternoon — even cutting themselves and bleeding profusely — in hopes that Baal would manifest and consume their sacrifice, but he never responded.

At the time of the evening sacrifice, Elijah arranged the sacrifice to God on the altar and had it and the wood drenched with water. He then prayed and asked God to show the people that He is the One True God by consuming the sacrifice with fire sent from Heaven. The Bible says, "Then the fire of the Lord fell and consumed the burnt sacrifice, and the wood and the stones and the dust, and it licked up the water that was in the trench. Now when all the people saw it, they fell on their faces; and they said, 'The Lord, He is God! The Lord, He is God!'" (1 Kings 18:38,39)

Immediately, Elijah mobilized the people of Israel and had them seize all 450 prophets of Baal and brought them to the Kishon Valley where they were slaughtered. Elijah then told Ahab that the three-and-a-half-year drought was coming to an end; rain was on the way. As Ahab got into his chariot and made his way home, Elijah tucked his cloak in his belt and outran Ahab's chariot, making it to Jezreel before him. Without question, this was one amazing day of ministry for Elijah.

God's Heart Is To Comfort and Strengthen Those Who Are Exhausted

In the meantime, "…Ahab told Jezebel all that Elijah had done, also how he had executed all the prophets with the sword. Then Jezebel sent a messenger to Elijah, saying, 'So let the gods do to me, and more also, if

I do not make your life as the life of one of them by tomorrow about this time'" (1 Kings 19:1,2).

When Elijah heard Jezebel's death threat, "…He arose and ran for his life, and went to Beersheba, which belongs to Judah, and left his servant there. But he himself went a day's journey into the wilderness, and came and sat down under a broom tree. And he prayed that he might die, and said, 'It is enough! Now, Lord, take my life, for I am no better than my fathers!'"
(1 Kings 19:3,4).

You may read this and think, *Wait a minute. Is this the same mighty man of God that called down fire from Heaven? Is this the prophet that put 450 prophets of Baal to the sword and then outran a chariot?* The answer is yes, it is. Why was he acting like this? The answer is simple: he was absolutely exhausted. When Elijah said he was no better than his ancestors and prayed that God would take his life, it was sheer exhaustion talking.

After flowing powerfully in the anointing of God, Elijah basically collapsed. Physically, mentally, and emotionally he was sapped of his strength, and after hearing Jezebel's threats against his life, discouragement and deep despair had taken a firm grip on his soul. Scripture says, "…As he lay and slept under a broom tree, suddenly an angel touched him, and said to him, 'Arise and eat.' Then he looked, and there by his head was a cake baked on coals, and a jar of water. So he ate and drank, and lay down again" (1 Kings 19:5,6).

Please notice that God didn't come and bring judgment to Elijah — He brought *comfort* in the form of warm food, refreshing drink, and sweet sleep. This is what Elijah needed most. If you are absolutely exhausted like Elijah, God is not waiting to criticize and judge you. He wants to comfort and strengthen you just as he did Elijah.

First Kings 19:7 and 8 goes on to say, "And the angel of the Lord came back the second time, and touched him, and said, 'Arise and eat, because the journey is too great for you.' So he arose, and ate and drank; and he went in the strength of that food forty days and forty nights as far as Horeb, the mountain of God." Again, we see that God was not ready to pounce on Elijah or put him down because he was defeated in spirit and struggling with unbelief. On the contrary, God came a second time to comfort and strengthen him and walk with him on the rest of his journey.

It wasn't time for Elijah to die; God had more for him to do. The same is true for you. You may be exhausted and thinking, *I don't know how I'm ever going to get through this. How's my loved one ever going to make it out of this situation? I just can't do this anymore.* But friend, no problem is too big for God! He doesn't want you to live in perpetual exhaustion. He wants to strengthen you by the power of His Spirit who is living inside you. He is the Unstoppable One, and through His strength, you can do all things (*see* Philippians 4:13).

God Lovingly Helps Us Regain Our Direction

When the angel of the Lord came and touched Elijah a second time, "…He [Elijah] arose, and ate and drank; and he went in the strength of that food forty days and forty nights as far as Horeb, the mountain of God" (1 Kings 19:8). Verse 9 explains, "And there he went into a cave, and spent the night in that place; and behold, the word of the Lord came to him, and He said to him, 'What are you doing here, Elijah?'"

Again, there was no judgment or criticism from God — just His comforting voice of love trying to help Elijah regain his footing and begin moving in the right direction. In some ways, this situation is similar to what Rick experienced many years ago when he was attempting to build a church in Riga, Latvia. Denise recounted the story, saying:

> It was an amazing, yet overwhelming project for my husband because he had to come up with money to pay the contractors again and again — sometimes for days on end. Rick just didn't know where he was going to get the money.
>
> One night, the financial situation reached a crisis level, and Rick was overwhelmed with worry. Unable to sleep, he got out of bed, made his way to the office, and dropped his head down on the desk in despair. He prayed, "God, I don't know what to do. Where's this money going to come from?"
>
> It was in that moment of desperation that our youngest son Joel awakened for some reason and got out of bed and walked down the hall into the office where he saw his dad with his head on the desk. "Dad, what are you doing here," he said. "What's wrong?"

With a wavering voice, Rick said, "Joel, I have these bills I need to pay for the new church, and I have no idea where I'm going to get the money to pay them."

"Aw, Dad," Joel replied, "Hasn't God done enough for you already to let you know that He's going to take care of you now?" Amazingly, God woke up our young son in the middle of the night and sent him to encourage and comfort — not condemn — Rick when he was struggling to trust God for the needed finances.

This is what we see God doing with Elijah as he was in the process of recovering from a time of intense warfare against evil forces that were trying to destroy his nation. Motivated by love, the Father saw him in the cave and said to him, "…What are you doing here, Elijah?" (1 Kings 19:9).

God Spoke Softly and Clearly to Elijah

In answer to God's question, Elijah said, "I have been very zealous for the Lord God of hosts; for the children of Israel have forsaken Your covenant, torn down Your altars, and killed Your prophets with the sword. I alone am left; and they seek to take my life" (1 Kings 19:10).

To this, God responded, "'…Go out, and stand on the mountain before the Lord'" (1 Kings 19:11). And the Word says, "And behold, the Lord passed by, and a great and strong wind tore into the mountains and broke the rocks in pieces before the Lord, but the Lord was not in the wind; and after the wind an earthquake, but the Lord was not in the earthquake; and after the earthquake a fire, but the Lord was not in the fire; and after the fire a still small voice" (1 Kings 19:11,12).

The strong wind, the earthquake, and the raging fire all represent the dramatic demonstrations of God's mighty power that Elijah was accustomed to seeing in his ministry. In this case, God was not speaking to Elijah through any of these spectacular displays. Instead, He chose to talk to Elijah using *a still small voice* — a quiet, gentle whisper that required Elijah to draw intimately close to God in order to hear Him.

First Kings 19:13 says, "So it was, when Elijah heard it, that he wrapped his face in his mantle and went out and stood in the entrance of the cave. Suddenly a voice came to him, and said, 'What are you doing here, Elijah?'" Almost word for word, Elijah answered a second time saying, "I have been very zealous for the Lord God of hosts; because the children of

Israel have forsaken Your covenant, torn down Your altars, and killed Your prophets with the sword. I alone am left; and they seek to take my life" (1 Kings 19:14).

Elijah Finished His Ministry in a Blaze of Fire

At this point, God began to speak candidly with Elijah — directing him to "Go" and anoint Hazael as king over Syria, Jehu as king over Israel, and Elisha as the prophet who would take his place (*see* 1 Kings 19:15,16). The Lord also set the record straight and informed Elijah that he was not the only loyal prophet left. He said, "I have reserved seven thousand in Israel, all whose knees have not bowed to Baal, and every mouth that has not kissed him" (1 Kings 19:18).

Elijah obeyed God's instructions and returned to finish the work he had been called to do. His encounter with God transformed his life — irradicating fear and reigniting boldness to carry out his assignments.

Although Elijah begged God twice to take his life, he never tasted death. Instead, he completed his course, literally being swept away in a whirlwind of fire! (*See* Second Kings 2:11.) Friend, if you're exhausted from all that you've been doing, seek the face of God and let Him infuse you with fresh fire. His promise through Isaiah still extends to you today: "He gives power to the faint and weary, and to him who has no might He increases strength [causing it to multiply and making it to abound]" (Isaiah 40:29 *AMPC*).

STUDY QUESTIONS

Study to shew thyself approved unto God, a workman that needeth not to be ashamed, rightly dividing the word of truth.
— 2 Timothy 2:15

1. God doesn't want you to live in perpetual exhaustion. He wants to strengthen you just as He strengthened Elijah by the power of His Spirit. How do you receive His strength? Consider what God says in the following passages and begin to draw upon the strength of His Spirit daily.

   - Isaiah 40:28-31; 41:10

   - Micah 3:8; Zechariah 4:6; Acts 1:8

   - Ephesians 3:16-21

- 2 Corinthians 12:9,10

- Philippians 4:13

2. Elijah's life is a reminder that in addition to feeding our spirit, all of us need to take care of our body and soul as well. What does God's Word have to say regarding this? Check out these verses — in a few Bible versions — for some answers.

   - Romans 12:1

   - 1 Corinthians 6:12-20

   - 2 Corinthians 7:1

3. Does it seem as though your situation is impossible to change? It's not…if you'll invite God into it! Read Jesus' extraordinary promise repeated in Matthew 19:26; Mark 9:23 and 10:27, along with God's encouraging words through Gabriel in Luke 1:37.

PRACTICAL APPLICATION

**But be ye doers of the word, and not hearers only,
deceiving your own selves.**
—James 1:22

1. In what ways can you identify with Elijah? Are you beyond exhausted, doing all you can do to raise and care for your children/grandchildren, maintain your home, and pay your bills? Are you caring for elderly parents, volunteering at church, or working multiple jobs to make ends meet? Get quiet in God's presence and allow Him to comfort you as He did Elijah. What is He speaking to your heart right now?

2. If you're feeling overwhelmed by multiple attacks on many fronts, don't believe the lie that it would be better for you to die. It wasn't true for Elijah, and it's not true for you. God has more for you to do. Take time to pray and pour your heart out to God (*see* Psalm 62:8). Humbly ask Him to infuse you with the power of His Spirit and to give you spiritual eyes to see things the way they really are. (*Consider* Second Kings 6:15-17.)

3. Clearly, Elijah was a powerful prophet of God, but he was not without flaws and weaknesses. Like all of us, he needed to care for his body and soul and have godly friends around him to help him through difficult times. Moving forward, what practical adjustments do you

sense the Lord prompting you to make in order to avoid the pitfalls of exhaustion and depression?

TOPIC

Jacob — From Deceiver to Prince With God

SYNOPSIS

One of the most memorable people in Scripture is a man named Jacob. He is the grandson of Abraham and second-born son of his father Isaac. Before becoming the father of the 12 tribes of Israel, Jacob was a deceitful schemer who manipulated people into getting what he wanted. Yet when he came face to face with the living God, his identity was transformed, and his life was launched in the direction of great destiny. A study of Jacob's life reveals that regardless of how you start, you can finish right with the transforming power of God.

The emphasis of this lesson:

The name "Jacob" means *schemer* or *deceiver*, which is exactly how he lived the first part of his life. But while working for his Uncle Laban, he reaped a hearty helping of the deception he had dished out. The night Jacob wrestled with the Lord, he came face to face with who he was. In that divine moment, God transformed him, changing him into Israel — *prince with God.*

The Holy Spirit Is the Agent of Transformation

Under the inspiration of the Holy Spirit, the apostle Paul wrote to the believers in Corinth, saying, "But we all, with unveiled face, beholding as in a mirror the glory of the Lord, are being transformed into the same image from glory to glory, just as by the Spirit of the Lord" (2 Corinthians 3:18).

This passage tells us that when we fix our eyes on Jesus — spending time in the Word, worshiping Him with all our heart, or experiencing His tangible presence in prayer — we're transformed into His image. This transformation is progressive, which means with each successive exposure to God's presence, we're changed from one level of His glory to the next.

Who does the transforming? It's the Holy Spirit who is living inside of you. That's why Paul prayed, "May the God of peace himself make you entirely pure and devoted to God; and may your spirit and soul and body be kept strong and blameless until that day when our Lord Jesus Christ comes back again. God, who called you to become his child, will do all this for you, just as he promised" (1 Thessalonians 5:23,24 *TLB*).

Friend, no time spent with God is wasted. Time in His presence always produces transformation.

Jacob Was a Schemer and Deceiver

Most of Jacob's life story is recorded in Genesis 25 through 35. What's interesting is that he is the fraternal twin brother of Esau, and from the moment he entered the world, he was fighting to get ahead of others. The Bible says that as his mother Rebekah was giving birth, Esau emerged first with Jacob grabbing hold of his brother's heel (*see* Genesis 25:26). That's how he got the name "Jacob," which means *supplanter — one who tries to oust, displace, or supersede another.*

By order of birth, Esau was the firstborn and entitled to all the blessings that came with that position. Jacob, however, took advantage of his brother and manipulated him into surrendering his birthright in exchange for a meal of stew. Even worse, when Jacob's father Isaac was old and blind, Jacob tricked him into thinking he was Esau so that Isaac would speak the blessing of the firstborn over him instead of his brother. With the help of Rebekah, Jacob succeeded in stealing Esau's blessing. This act caused Esau to hate Jacob — so much so that Rebekah told him, "…Surely your brother Esau comforts himself concerning you by intending to kill you" (Genesis 27:42).

Upon hearing this news, Jacob heeded his mother's direction and fled for his life to Haran where he began working for his Uncle Laban. This was the beginning of nearly two decades of Jacob reaping the same type of deceptive treatment he had dished out to his brother and father. For instance, Laban promised Jacob his daughter Rachel's hand in marriage, but on the night of their wedding, he gave Jacob his older daughter Leah instead. Jacob was made to work another seven years before he could wed

Rachel. Add to this, there were multiple times that Laban stole Jacob's flocks and manipulated situations to his advantage. Indeed, when Jacob met Laban, he had finally met his match.

Jacob Comes Face to Face With His Deception

The day finally came when Jacob and his family broke free from Laban's lair of deception and began to make their way back to his homeland. Of course, this meant Jacob would have to face his brother Esau and come to grips with all the mean and deceptive things he had done to him. The thought of this reunion terrified Jacob. In fact, when he learned that Esau and 400 of his men were traveling to meet him, the Bible says, "…Jacob was greatly afraid and distressed; and he divided the people that were with him, and the flocks and herds and camels, into two companies. And he said, 'If Esau comes to the one company and attacks it, then the other company which is left will escape'" (Genesis 32:7,8).

Someone may read Jacob's story and think, *Well, Esau chose to sell his birthright, and Jacob's mom was the one who devised a plan to deceive Isaac. It's not all Jacob's fault.* Although this is true, we need to see what God has to say about someone who exhibits the negative character traits of Jacob. Few passages speak more clearly on what God thinks of people who lie, cheat, and steal than Proverbs 6:16-19. It says:

> **These six things the Lord hates, yes, seven are an abomination to Him:**
>
> **A proud look, a lying tongue, hands that shed innocent blood,**
>
> **A heart that devises wicked plans, feet that are swift in running to evil,**
>
> **A false witness who speaks lies, and one who sows discord among brethren.**

One who lies, devises wicked plans, and operates in pride is an abomination in God's eyes. To receive and live under God's blessing, Jacob had to repent to God of his deceptive ways and allow Him to do a deep, restorative work in his heart. Clearly, the impending encounter with Esau was the circumstance Jacob needed to drive him to his knees and make things right with God.

The Lord Wrestled With Jacob

As Jacob prepared to face his estranged brother, he earnestly prayed, "…O God of my father Abraham and God of my father Isaac, the Lord who said to me, 'Return to your country and to your family, and I will deal well with you': I am not worthy of the least of all the mercies and of all the truth which You have shown Your servant; for I crossed over this Jordan with my staff, and now I have become two companies. Deliver me, I pray, from the hand of my brother, from the hand of Esau; for I fear him, lest he come and attack me and the mother with the children. For You said, 'I will surely treat you well, and make your descendants as the sand of the sea, which cannot be numbered for multitude'" (Genesis 32:9-12).

In this passage, we see that the pressure of the impending meeting with Esau has broken Jacob's pride, causing him to repent and to humble himself before God. At the same time, we see him exercise his faith and begin to remind the Lord of His promises, which he was holding on to tenaciously.

Shortly thereafter, Jacob divided his children and wives into two groups and sent them across the Jabbok River ahead of him. The Bible says, "Then Jacob was left alone; and a Man wrestled with him until the breaking of day" (Genesis 32:24). Many scholars believe that this Man was a preincarnate manifestation of Jesus who came to wrestle with Jacob, which seems most likely.

Scripture goes on to say, "…When He [the Lord] saw that He did not prevail against him [Jacob], He touched the socket of his hip; and the socket of Jacob's hip was out of joint as He wrestled with him" (Genesis 32:25). Isn't that amazing? The Creator of the universe took on the form of man and came down to earth to wrestle with Jacob — a man who had a reputation for being a liar and deceiver.

When God saw Jacob and the terrible dilemma he was in, He chose to come down and wrestle with him. If you stop to think about it, Jesus did the same thing for us. When He saw our dreadful, sinful condition, He humbled Himself, took on the form of man, and wrestled with His own will in the Garden of Gethsemane. Throughout that agonizing conflict, He defeated His flesh and came under the authority of the Father, yielding His life to the excruciating death of the Cross.

Friend, this demonstrates how the love of God will stop at no bounds to reach you, to touch you, and to save you. He will move Heaven and earth to deliver you and those you love from addictions, poisonous relationships, or any other terrible situation.

Jacob Came Face to Face With Who He Was

The story continues in Genesis 32:26, where the Lord said, "'Let Me go, for the day breaks.' But he [Jacob] said, 'I will not let You go unless You bless me!'" Apparently, Jacob had been wrestling with the Lord in the darkness of night, and the Lord needed to leave before the sun came up and revealed His identity.

In response, the Lord said to Jacob, "'…What is your name?' He said, 'Jacob'" (Genesis 32:27). In that moment, Jacob had to come face to face with who he had been. When he responded, "Jacob," it was as if he was telling the Lord, "I'm a trickster! I'm a deceiver! I've been trying to supplant others since the moment of my birth."

The Lord answered Jacob's desperate cry of brokenness by saying, "…Your name shall no longer be called Jacob, but *Israel*; for you have struggled with God and with men, and have prevailed" (Genesis 32:28). In that divine encounter with God, Jacob experienced an amazing transformation. No longer would he be called trickster, swindler, or deceiver (Jacob). God changed his name to Israel, which means *prince with God.*

Clearly, the Lord won the wrestling match, but Jacob held on and received a blessing just as he requested. That blessing was a brand-new identity. Here again, we see that when the presence of God shows up in a person's life, that person never leaves the same!

The God of the Impossible
Can Handle Your Impossible Situation

Like Jacob, Denise faced a time in her life when she too wrestled with God for something she needed. Here's what she shared:

> I was in a critical situation, dealing with physical challenges going on in my body, and it was seriously affecting my mind. Intense fear and anxiety came against me, and I didn't know what to do. Although I appreciate and respect the gift of doctors, I just didn't have peace about going to them about this condition. I didn't

want to begin taking a bunch of pills or be poked and prodded through a barrage of endless tests. I just didn't want to go there.

The fact is, I had already been touched and healed by God many years earlier, so I was determined in my heart to seek Him and wait on Him to heal me again. Although I didn't know it, there were things He needed to do in me — changes that needed to take place that could only come about while I was in my current challenging circumstances.

Through it all, I continued to hold tightly to the Lord and the promises in His Word. I remember one night when I was deeply upset that I grabbed hold of the sink and said, 'God, I don't know what's going on in my life, and I don't know what I need to do. You know how miserable I am, but I'm not letting go of You until you change me.' Looking back, I'm so glad I held on and didn't let go. Like Jacob, God blessed my life in indescribable ways and brought me through the hardships I'd been facing.

Friend, if God will wrestle with a man who was a liar and a deceiver and give him a brand-new identity, He will certainly help *you*! Again, there are no limits to what He can do. The Bible says, "…God demonstrates His own love toward us, in that while we were still sinners, Christ died for us" (Romans 5:8). Jesus took our punishment — enduring the Roman scourging, the excruciating Crucifixion, and a descent into hell itself — all to ransom us and pay the price for our sins. He was gloriously raised to life on the third day, and now He intercedes for us continually in prayer as our Great High Priest.

What an amazing and indescribable love God has for us! It knows no boundaries and can break through any barriers to touch and transform anyone — regardless of his or her condition. So, you're not helpless or hopeless. You can believe for the impossible because God is the God of the impossible. Indeed, "God can do anything, you know — far more than you could ever imagine or guess or request in your wildest dreams!" (Ephesians 3:20 *MSG*)

As you seek and surrender yourself to the Holy Spirit — who lives in you — He will touch and transform your life with His power like nothing and no one else can. Open your heart and mind to Him and say, "God, Your presence is here, and I ask You to change me. I acknowledge that I'm powerless to change myself, but as I fix my eyes on You and dig deep into

Your Word, You will transform me just as You transformed Jacob. I ask this in Jesus' name. Amen!"

STUDY QUESTIONS

Study to shew thyself approved unto God, a workman that needeth not to be ashamed, rightly dividing the word of truth.
— 2 Timothy 2:15

1. In the early years of his life, Jacob was a schemer and deceiver, manipulating people and things to get what he wanted. Do you have someone like Jacob in your life? Are you yourself like Jacob? What sobering truth does God give us in Galatians 6:7 and 8 that should move us to pray for God's mercy for anyone in Jacob's shoes? (Also consider Job 4:8; Proverbs 22:8; and Luke 6:38.)

2. The fact that the Lord changed Jacob's name to *Israel* is quite remarkable. Can you think of anyone else in Scripture whose name was changed? Consider the people in these passages. What do you think the significance and purpose is behind their name changes?

   • Genesis 17:1-8,15,16

   • Judges 6:28-32

   • 2 Samuel 12:24,25

   • Matthew 16:17,18

3. What does Jesus Himself say in Revelation 2:17 and 3:12 that He is going to do in the future for you as you live your life to bring Him glory? How does this encourage you?

PRACTICAL APPLICATION

But be ye doers of the word, and not hearers only, deceiving your own selves.
—James 1:22

1. Like Jacob, have you ever had to return and face a person or situation you ran from? If so, describe what took place. Why did you leave in the first place, and what made you turn back and face the situation head-on? In the end, how did God use the confrontation to heal and transform your life and the lives of others?

2. As Jacob prepared to face his brother Esau, he reminded the Lord of the promises He had given him. Isaiah 62:6 (*AMPC*) says, "…You who [are His servants and by your prayers] put the Lord in remembrance [of His promises], keep not silence." What promises has the Lord given you that you need to remind yourself of and begin praying about once again?

3. As you come to the close of this lesson, is the Holy Spirit showing you any ungodly tendencies in your character you need to face? If so, take them straight to God in prayer right now. Ask Him to forgive you and give you His grace to abandon that old, carnal way of thinking and be transformed by the power of His Spirit.

TOPIC

Gideon — From Hidden to Hero

SYNOPSIS

Do you feel as though you're invisible or hidden from the eyes of others? You're not alone. There are many people in Scripture who were concealed by God, including a man by the name of Gideon. Yet at just the right moment, God brought transformation to him and elevated him from obscurity, giving him a special assignment to push back the enemies of darkness and deliver His people from danger. That same kind of transformation power is available to you! Indeed, God has a divine assignment with *your* name on it, and at just the right time, He'll move you out of obscurity into the limelight to tackle the specific tasks He has called you to do!

The emphasis of this lesson:

Gideon was called to lead the nation of Israel and defeat the oppressing Midianite forces. Initially, he had a very belittling view of himself and was filled with fear. But when the Lord showed up and empowered Gideon with His Spirit, he was transformed into a bold warrior who obeyed God's instructions and defeated Israel's enemies.

People Are Transformed
When God's Presence Shows Up

In our first lesson, we learned about the Egyptian girl Hagar and how she ran from Sarai because she was being treated so harshly. God met Hagar in a time of deep desperation and gave her direction and divine hope for her future.

In Lesson 2, we talked about the prophet Elijah and how after an outstanding day of victorious ministry he fell into exhaustion and deep depression. Rather than judging Elijah for giving into fear and unbelief, God comforted him by providing him with food and deep sleep. Once he was rested and ready, God gave Elijah the direction he needed to get up and get moving again.

In our last lesson, we looked at the life of Jacob, whose name means *trickster*, *deceiver*, or *schemer*. Although he had lied and manipulated people to get his way, God brought him to a place of brokenness and total dependence on Him. Great transformation came to Jacob the night he wrestled with the Lord. During his supernatural skirmish, the Lord changed his name from swindler and deceiver to "Israel" — *prince with God.*

What amazing compassion our God has! His love is indescribable and will stop at nothing to reach and restore us. Indeed, "…If God is for us, who [can be] against us? [Who can be our foe, if God is on our side?]" (Romans 8:31 *AMPC*). Friend, there's no mountain too high or valley too low that God can't reach you and those you love. And if He has touched your life in the past, He will touch your life — and the lives of your loved ones — again. Physical healing, relational restoration, financial provision, and so much more are all available to you through Jesus.

The Lord Made a Surprise Appearance to Gideon

After the death of Joshua, the nation of Israel entered a time when they were ruled by judges that God raised up from among His people. One such judge was a man by the name of Gideon. The Lord called him during a period when the Israelites were in rebellion against Him and worshiping false gods. As a result of their disobedience, the Lord delivered them into the hands of the Midianites (*see* Judges 6:1).

Scripture says that the people of Midian were stealing Israel's crops and livestock, leaving them greatly impoverished. Out of desperation, the Israelites cried out to the Lord, and the Lord sent a prophet to the children of Israel, who said to them, "…Thus says the Lord God of Israel: 'I brought you up from Egypt and brought you out of the house of bondage; and I delivered you out of the hand of the Egyptians and out of the hand of all who oppressed you, and drove them out before you and gave you their land. Also I said to you, "I am the Lord your God; do not fear the gods of the Amorites, in whose land you dwell." But you have not obeyed My voice'" (Judges 6:8-10).

Isn't it amazing how we will turn to God when we're in trouble and our world seems to be falling apart? Nothing seems to capture our undivided attention like coming face to face with catastrophe, and that is exactly where the children of Israel were. It was at their point of desperation that the Bible says the Angel of the Lord made a surprise appearance to Gideon while he was secretly threshing wheat in his family's winepress (*see* Judges 6:11). Scripture says:

> **And the Angel of the Lord appeared to him, and said to him, "The Lord is with you, you mighty man of valor!"**
>
> **Gideon said to Him, "O my lord, if the Lord is with us, why then has all this happened to us? And where are all His miracles which our fathers told us about, saying, 'Did not the Lord bring us up from Egypt?' But now the Lord has forsaken us and delivered us into the hands of the Midianites."**
>
> **Then the Lord turned to him and said, "Go in this might of yours, and you shall save Israel from the hand of the Midianites. Have I not sent you?"**
>
> **So he said to Him, "O my Lord, how can I save Israel? Indeed my clan is the weakest in Manasseh, and I am the least in my father's house."**
>
> **And the Lord said to him, "Surely I will be with you, and you shall defeat the Midianites as one man."**
>
> **—Judges 6:12-16**

Gideon Had a Hard Time Believing What God Said About Him

It's important to point out that the Angel of the Lord in this passage is once again a preincarnate manifestation of the Lord Himself as we will see in a few moments. Also note what the Lord says to Gideon: He calls him a "mighty man of valor" and then prophesies victory over the Midianites by his hand.

In Gideon's mind, this prediction is just too far-fetched for him to believe, which is why he basically replies, "Oh, that's not me; I'm the runt of my family, and our tribe is the least of all in Israel. You have the wrong person."

Can you identify with Gideon? Has God ever commissioned you to do something, and you said, "Oh, no God. You must be confusing me with someone else. That's not me. I can't speak (or sing, cook, act, etc.) like so and so. I just don't have what it takes to do what You're asking." This type of comparing ourselves with others is unhealthy. In fact, Second Corinthians 10:12 (*AMPC*) says when people "…measure themselves with themselves and compare themselves with one another, they are without understanding and behave unwisely."

Friend, God only made *one* of you, and you are so amazing! You can see for yourself in Psalm 139. Out of eight billion people on the planet, no one has your eyes, your voice, your fingerprints, or your DNA. Furthermore, God has equipped you to do something special, and that's what He was telling Gideon.

When God chose Gideon, He knew exactly what He was doing and what He was getting. He knew all of Gideon's gifts and strengths as well as his faults and weaknesses, and He knows the same things about you. God loved Gideon so much that He came to him personally and told him, "You are a mighty man of valor! And you're going to bring down those Midianites!"

What Do You Think About Yourself?

The Bible says, "For as he (a man) thinks in his heart, so is he…" (Proverbs 23:7). In other words, what you think about yourself is what you become, and with the thousands of thoughts that fill your brain every day, it is vital to periodically stop and give thought to what you think about yourself.

If you think and believe thoughts that you're unworthy, incapable, and unlovable, then that's what you'll be. If you think you're lacking, less than, or the least, then that's what you will experience. You literally are what you think. That's why it's crucial for you to renew your mind with the truth of God's Word and begin to think and believe what He says about you. When you believe and speak what God says, you come into agreement with Him and position yourself to succeed at anything and everything He calls you to do.

When we read between the lines of Gideon's response, we see that he wrongly believed and told the Lord he was…

- Unable to do what God called him to do, which was to save Israel from the Midianites.

- From the least significant family in Israel.

- The smallest and weakest of all his family members.

Do any of these arguments sound like something you've thought or said about yourself? Friend, if you're telling yourself you're weak, powerless, unacceptable, or unable to do what God is asking you to do, stop it and stop it now!

Begin to think and say what God thinks and says about you. For instance, God says:

- You're a brand-new creation in Christ Jesus!
  (*See* Second Corinthians 5:17.)

- You're acceptable to God in Christ! (*See* Ephesians 1:6.)

- You are the righteousness of God in Christ Jesus!
  (*See* Second Corinthians 5:21.)

- You are strong in the Lord in the power of His might!
  (*See* Ephesians 6:10.)

- You can do all things through Christ who gives you strength!
  (*See* Philippians 4:13.)

- You're the head and not the tail; you're above and not beneath!
  (*See* Deuteronomy 28:13.)

You are all these things in Christ and so much more! Why? Because God said so!

Accepting What God Says About You and Accepting His Assignment Is Often a Process

To ensure that he was really hearing from God and that he had God's favor, Gideon asked Him for a confirming sign. Specifically, he asked the Lord to wait for him to prepare and offer a sacrifice, which is exactly what the Lord did. When Gideon had everything ready, the Lord produced fire from the rock on which the sacrifice sat and utterly consumed it (*see* Judges 6:17-21). The Lord was not frustrated or put out by Gideon's request. He saw Gideon's willing heart to obey and provided the confirming sign he needed.

Immediately after the sacrifice was consumed and the Lord vanished, Gideon humbled himself before God and built an altar to commemorate His visit. The Lord then spoke to Gideon and directed him to tear down his father's altar to Baal and build an altar to the Lord in its place. Gideon came into agreement and obeyed God's instructions, which took a great deal of courage. Indeed, it was an audacious and bold act to demolish and incinerate his own father's idols.

When the men of the city found out what Gideon had done, they demanded he be executed. But God protected Gideon from all harm and continued to declare that he would defeat the Midianites. For his heroic act, Gideon was given a new name — the name Jerubbaal, which means *let Baal plead for himself* (*see* Judges 6:31,32). Gideon had courageously stood against Baal and prevailed, and from that day forward he was called by his new name.

Although it may seem strange, Gideon was still dealing with uncertainty. Consequently, he asked God for two additional signs to confirm that he would have victory against the Midianites. The Lord graciously provided both "fleeces" that Gideon requested (*see* Judges 6:36-40), and with a renewed certainty of victory, he moved forward to carry out the Lord's assignment.

If you read through Judges 7, you'll discover that God told Gideon he had too many soldiers with him. The Lord then systematically weeded out certain people, reducing the size of Israel's army from 22,000 men to 300 men. That's all God needed to defeat the Midianite army — 300 sold-out soldiers who walked in sync with Him.

As Gideon got into agreement with what God said about him, God empowered him to carry out his assignment. He destroyed his father's idols, rallied a group of warriors, and defeated the Midianites in the matchless might of the One True God!

You Have God's Resurrection Power in You!

Be encouraged, friend! If Gideon was victorious in his God-given assignment, you will be victorious in yours. But unlike Gideon, you have the Person of the Holy Spirit living inside you — not just with you — and His resurrection power is greater than all the power of the enemy. First John 4:4 says, "…He who is in you is greater than he who is in the world." Notice it's not the lesser one that lives in you — it's *the Greater One*. And He's greater than anything you'll ever face in this world.

Who are the "Midianites" in your life right now? What are they trying to do to you and your family? What intimidating words are they saying? Whatever the case may be, do not fear the gods of this world! They may threaten to take your job or persecute you in some way but pay them no mind. In Christ, "…we are more than conquerors through Him who loved us" (Romans 8:37).

So begin to line up your thinking with God's Word, and start saying what He says about you. The resurrection power of God on the inside of you is well able to take down any lie, any false accusation, and any enemy coming against you! Like Gideon, you can stand up against any enemy and experience victory through the empowering grace of Jesus Christ!

STUDY QUESTIONS

> **Study to shew thyself approved unto God, a workman that needeth not to be ashamed, rightly dividing the word of truth.**
> **— 2 Timothy 2:15**

1. Disobedience comes with a price, and the Israelites were paying a high cost for their ungodly choices. Thankfully, God is merciful and provides a path or restoration back into right relationship with Him. According to First John 1:9; Acts 2:38 and 3:19, what is the right,

God-ordained way we're to respond when we have sinned and disobeyed Him? (Also consider Proverbs 28:13 and Psalm 32:1-6.)

2. When you choose to walk in obedience, you position yourself to receive God's blessing! What can you expect to happen when you obey the Lord? Consider what He says in these passages.

    - Isaiah 1:19

    - Exodus 19:5,6; 20:6

    - 1 Kings 3:14

    - James 1:22-25

    - Deuteronomy 28:1-14

3. You are one of a kind! No one else on planet Earth is like you. David understood this truth and was moved by God's Spirit to write about it in Psalm 139:1-18. As you take time to carefully reflect on this passage, what are the things God knows about you? What does this tell you about your flaws and weaknesses and the times you sin and fall short of His standard?

PRACTICAL APPLICATION

**But be ye doers of the word, and not hearers only,
deceiving your own selves.
—James 1:22**

1. What has God been talking to you about and asking you to do? Is it starting a business, stepping out into ministry, or relocating your family? How have you responded to His direction? Have you ignored or dismissed His instructions? Or have you responded with doubt and fear like Gideon? If so, what obstacles are you focused on? What's keeping you from obeying God's instructions and experiencing His victory in your life?

2. When the Lord appeared to Gideon, he saw himself as the most insignificant member of his family and the weakest among the tribe of Manasseh. Yet God called Gideon a "mighty man of valor." Be honest: How do you see yourself? Has God spoken something to you that you find very difficult to believe and receive? If so, what has He said? Ask Him for grace to believe what he says about you.

3. Take time to review the section that lists the things God says about you in His Word. Pray and ask Him to help you to begin to *think and say* what He thinks and says about you! Remember, "Death and life are in the power of *your* tongue (*see* Proverbs 18:21). If you speak life, you will experience life.

TOPIC

Nebuchadnezzar — From Arrogant King to Worshiper of God

SYNOPSIS

There are many examples in Scripture of God transforming the lives of His people. But what about unbelievers? Does God ever transform the lives of individuals who are *not* following Him? The answer is *yes*, and one of the most unlikely people in history to be transformed is a Babylonian king named Nebuchadnezzar. A careful look at Scripture reveals how God used a series of situations to capture the attention of this arrogant, narcissistic ruler and transform him into a genuine worshiper of God. Let's unpack some of his story from the book of Daniel.

The emphasis of this lesson:

Nebuchadnezzar was quite a terror in his day, especially to the nation of Israel. Yet through the steadfast faith and obedience of Daniel and his three Hebrew friends, the Lord softened this proud, pagan king's heart, eventually transforming him into a servant of God who gave praise, glory, and honor to His holy Name.

The Transformer Lives in You!

Looking one last time at our anchor verse in Second Corinthians 3:18, it says, "But we all, with unveiled face, beholding as in a mirror the glory of the Lord, are being transformed into the same image from glory to glory, just as by the Spirit of the Lord."

We've noted that when you surrender your life to Jesus, you are saved, and the Spirit of God comes to live inside you. From that divine moment forward, the Bible declares, "…You are the temple of the living God…" (2 Corinthians 6:16). The Holy Spirit takes up permanent residence in you and begins transforming you into the likeness of Jesus. He is the supernatural agent of change! When you spend time in God's Word, worship Him from your heart, or simply meditate on His magnificence, an indescribable transformation takes place.

Every time God shows up in someone's life, they are no longer the same. We've seen this in the lives of Hagar, Elijah, Jacob, and Gideon, which we've examined in our previous lessons. God's presence opens our eyes to our true identity in Him and gives us the strength and direction we desperately need to move forward and fulfill our destiny. As we fix our eyes on Jesus, we're transformed into His glorious image in ever-increasing degrees.

God's People Were Taken Captive

Throughout the Old Testament, there is a very distinct pattern in the lives of the children of Israel: they went from serving God with great devotion to turning away from Him in rebellion and worshiping idols. We saw this in the time of the judges, and it was also the case during the reign of King Nebuchadnezzar. In fact, the Israelites had become so corrupt that the Lord allowed them to be taken into captivity in Babylon.

The book of Daniel traces some of the events that took place during that era, especially in the lives of Belteshazzar, Shadrach, Meshach, and Abed-Nego. But these were not their original names. According to Scripture, the Hebrew names of these young nobles were Daniel, Hananiah, Mishael, and Azariah respectively. They were reassigned pagan names in an effort to change their identity. Not only did these young men lose their names, but they also lost their Hebrew culture, their families, and their homeland. Yet through it all, they didn't lose their relationship with God.

The lives of these four young leaders became powerful instruments in God's hands through which He commanded the attention of Nebuchadnezzar. Little by little, event after event, God revealed to this proud, pagan king His will and His ways and drew the king's heart toward Himself.

Daniel Was Given an Opportunity
To Demonstrate God's Greatness

The first thing God used to get Nebuchadnezzar's attention was a series
of troubling dreams, which he experienced in the second year of his reign.
The Bible says they were so disturbing that he couldn't remember them.
Accordingly, "…the king gave the command to call the magicians, the
astrologers, the sorcerers, and the Chaldeans to tell the king his dreams.
So they came and stood before the king" (Daniel 2:2).

Nebuchadnezzar then demanded that his mystic counselors tell him both
the dream and its interpretation, and if they failed to do so, all of them
would be cut in pieces and their houses burned to the ground. Upon
hearing the king's decree, the Babylonian astrologers and magicians
pleaded with him to tell them his dream, declaring, "…There is no other
who can tell it to the king except the gods, whose dwelling is not with
flesh" (Daniel 2:11).

This response infuriated Nebuchadnezzar, and he gave the order to
begin killing all the wisemen of Babylon. When the authorities came
to kill Daniel and his three companions, Daniel humbly went to the
king and asked him for some time. The Bible says, "Then Daniel went
to his house, and made the decision known to Hananiah, Mishael, and
Azariah, his companions, that they might seek mercies from the God of
heaven concerning this secret, so that Daniel and his companions might
not perish with the rest of the wise men of Babylon. Then the secret was
revealed to Daniel in a night vision. So Daniel blessed the God of heaven"
(Daniel 2:17-19).

God Gave Nebuchadnezzar a Dream
Detailing the World's Major Empires

When you read Daniel 2:24-45, you'll see that Nebuchadnezzar's dream
is a prophetic picture of all the major empires that would rise and fall
throughout the history of the world — starting with Nebuchadnezzar
and the Babylonian kingdom, which was represented in his dream by the
golden head of the statue.

After Daniel correctly described the dream and gave its interpretation,
"…King Nebuchadnezzar fell on his face, prostrate before Daniel, and
commanded that they should present an offering and incense to him. The

king answered Daniel, and said, 'Truly your God is the God of gods, the Lord of kings, and a revealer of secrets, since you could reveal this secret.' Then the king promoted Daniel and gave him many great gifts; and he made him ruler over the whole province of Babylon, and chief administrator over all the wise men of Babylon" (Daniel 2:46-48).

Someone may ask, "Why in the world would God give a wicked, proud, pagan king a prophetic dream detailing all the world's major empires and the culmination of the age?" More than likely it was because God was trying to get a hold of Nebuchadnezzar's heart. Keep in mind, the Lord loves everyone and doesn't want anyone to spend eternity separated from Him.

God Revealed Himself to Nebuchadnezzar When the Three Hebrew Youths Were Thrown Into the Fire

Shortly after the king's dream was interpreted, Nebuchadnezzar got the idea to build a golden image that towered approximately 90 feet into the air. He gathered all his officials together and announced that everyone in his kingdom — all nationalities and all languages — was to fall down and worship the image when they heard the symphony of music begin to play. Anyone who didn't prostrate themselves and worship was to be cast into a burning fiery furnace (*see* Daniel 3:1-6).

You probably remember what happened. Shadrach, Meshach, and Abed-Nego — Daniel's closest friends — refused to bow down and worship, so the king became infuriated and had them thrown into the fiery furnace, giving orders to turn the heat up seven times hotter. The fire was so hot it killed the king's men who threw the Hebrew youths into the furnace. But what happened next can only be described as miraculous.

> **Then King Nebuchadnezzar was astonished; and he rose in haste and spoke, saying to his counselors, "Did we not cast three men bound into the midst of the fire?" They answered and said to the king, "True, O king."**
>
> **"Look!" he answered, "I see four men loose, walking in the midst of the fire; and they are not hurt, and the form of the fourth is like the Son of God."**

> **Then Nebuchadnezzar went near the mouth of the burning
> fiery furnace and spoke, saying, "Shadrach, Meshach, and
> Abed-Nego, servants of the Most High God, come out, and
> come here." Then Shadrach, Meshach, and Abed-Nego came
> from the midst of the fire.**
>
> — Daniel 3:24-26

Here we see the presence of God Himself showing up right in the midst of the fire with Daniel's three friends. It's interesting to note that the visual manifestation of the Lord in Shadrach, Meshach, and Abed-Nego's life brought transformation to Nebuchadnezzar. His fury faded and his anger was abated when he saw Jesus in the flames.

Amazingly, when the three Hebrew youths came out of the intense inferno, the fire had no effect on them, and they didn't even smell like smoke! This miracle impacted the king so powerfully that the Bible says:

> **Nebuchadnezzar spoke, saying, "Blessed be the God of
> Shadrach, Meshach, and Abed-Nego, who sent His Angel
> and delivered His servants who trusted in Him, and they have
> frustrated the king's word, and yielded their bodies, that they
> should not serve nor worship any god except their own God!**
>
> **Therefore I make a decree that any people, nation, or language
> which speaks anything amiss against the God of Shadrach,
> Meshach, and Abed-Nego shall be cut in pieces, and their
> houses shall be made an ash heap; because there is no other
> God who can deliver like this."**
>
> — Daniel 3:28,29

Are you seeing and hearing what was happening in Nebuchadnezzar's life? This arrogant, pagan king was blessing and praising God! In front of all his officials, he verbally acknowledged that there is no other God like Jehovah — the God of Shadrach, Meshach, and Abed-Nego. All these responses from the king are tangible indicators that God was indeed at work transforming his heart and mind.

Nebuchadnezzar Was Given Another Dream Prophesying His Demise and Return to Power

After the Lord rescued Daniel's friends from the fiery furnace, Nebuchadnezzar promoted them to even higher positions of authority in Babylon.

Time passed, and once more the king's pride and arrogance began to get the better of him, and he became enamored with his own greatness. To this, God responded by giving Nebuchadnezzar another prophetic dream — this time describing what would happen to him in the not-so-distant future.

What is quite remarkable about this dream is that it is described by Nebuchadnezzar himself and recorded in the pages of Scripture. According to Nebuchadnezzar, it was written "…to declare the signs and wonders that the Most High God has worked for me" (Daniel 4:2). In the dream, the king saw a tree that grew up to the sky. It was strong and healthy, and both the birds of the air and the beasts of the field benefitted from it.

Suddenly, an order was given by a heavenly watcher to chop the tree down, leaving nothing but the stump and the roots. The dream then shifts, and the stump of the tree is likened to a man whose heart and mind become like that of an animal. For seven years he is sentenced to eat grass and roam the fields like a beast of the earth, "…in order that the living may know that the Most High rules in the kingdom of men, gives it to whomever He will, and sets over it the lowest of men" (Daniel 4:17).

Once Nebuchadnezzar told his dream to Daniel, the Lord enabled him to interpret it and explain it to the king. The great tree, whose height reached the heavens and could be seen by all the earth, was Nebuchadnezzar. Because of his great pride in thinking his kingdom was a result of his own efforts, God gave the order to cut him down to size and drive him out from among men to live among the beasts of the field. He was sentenced to eat grass and live like an animal for seven years until he knew and acknowledged "…that the Most High rules in the kingdom of men, and gives it to whomever he chooses" (Daniel 4:25).

Through Unprecedented Hardship Nebuchadnezzar Was Transformed Into a Servant of God

Within 12 months, the dream God gave Nebuchadnezzar came true with pinpoint accuracy. As the king was walking through his palace, once again boasting of his greatness, a voice from Heaven was suddenly heard. It decreed the precise judgment on Nebuchadnezzar that he was warned of in the dream one year earlier.

The Bible says, "That very hour the word was fulfilled concerning Nebuchadnezzar; he was driven from men and ate grass like oxen; his body was wet with the dew of heaven till his hair had grown like eagles' feathers and his nails like birds' claws" (Daniel 4:33).

It should be noted that upon delivering the interpretation of the dream, Daniel had urged the king, "…Stop sinning and do what is right. Break from your wicked past and be merciful to the poor. Perhaps then you will continue to prosper" (Daniel 4:27 *NLT*). Sadly, Nebuchadnezzar didn't repent of his pride or change his wicked ways, and therefore, he reaped the consequences of his own evil behavior. For seven years, history documents that he lived like a beast among the animals, just as the Lord had predicted.

Here is the king's personal account recorded in Daniel 4:34-37:

And at the end of the time I, Nebuchadnezzar, lifted my eyes to heaven, and my understanding returned to me; and I blessed the Most High and praised and honored Him who lives forever:

> **For His dominion is an everlasting dominion, and His kingdom is from generation to generation.**
>
> **All the inhabitants of the earth are reputed as nothing; He does according to His will in the army of heaven and among the inhabitants of the earth.**
>
> **No one can restrain His hand or say to Him, "What have You done?"**

At the same time my reason returned to me, and for the glory of my kingdom, my honor and splendor returned to me. My counselors and nobles resorted to me, I was restored to my kingdom, and excellent majesty was added to me.

Now I, Nebuchadnezzar, praise and extol and honor the King of heaven, all of whose works are truth, and His ways justice. And those who walk in pride He is able to put down.

Can you imagine it! This wicked, arrogant king was transformed into a worshiper of God. With his own mouth, he declared that there is no one who has higher authority that the Most High God. This was a true transformation indeed, and it demonstrates, yet again, that God will go to any lengths and bulldoze every barrier to touch the heart of a man or woman and transform them into a new creation! That's what He did with Nebuchadnezzar, and that's what He'll do with you and those you love.

STUDY QUESTIONS

Study to shew thyself approved unto God, a workman that needeth not to be ashamed, rightly dividing the word of truth.
— 2 Timothy 2:15

1. If anyone seemed an unlikely candidate to give God praise and worship, it would certainly have been King Nebuchadnezzar. Yet, what does God call him repeatedly in Jeremiah 25:9; 27:6; and 43:10?

2. What present-day, high-profile officials can you think of that seem extremely unlikely to honor God and turn their lives over to Him? What does First Timothy 2:1-4 say we are to do for these leaders? Are you doing it? (As you answer, consider what God says about those in authority through the apostle Paul in Romans 13:1-7.)

3. Take a few moments to reflect on Nebuchadnezzar's words in Daniel 2:47; 3:28; and 4:34-37. According to Luke 6:45 and Matthew 12:34, what do these words from the king's mouth tell us about the king's heart?

PRACTICAL APPLICATION

But be ye doers of the word, and not hearers only, deceiving your own selves.
— James 1:22

1. Prior to this lesson, what was your perception of King Nebuchadnezzar? Had you ever seen this God-honoring side of him before? Were you aware of the fact that his own words are recorded in Scripture (Daniel 4), and that he ended his kingdom giving wholehearted praise and glory to God, declaring Him to be "…the king of heaven, all of whose works are truth, and His ways justice" (Daniel 4:37)?

2. The Bible says, "He who heeds instruction and correction is [not only himself] in the way of life [but also] is a way of life for others…" (Proverbs 10:17 *AMPC*). Daniel, Shadrach, Meshach, and Abed-Nego were a way of life for King Nebuchadnezzar, paving the way for him to enter a relationship with the One True God. Be honest: When

people observe your life, what do they see? Is it *a way of life* leading them to Jesus? Or is it a confusing life of compromise that looks no different than a nonbeliever in the world?

3. Imagine you're alone at home, and Jesus walks into the room where you are. Your eyes suddenly lock eyes with His. What do you think He'd say to you about your witness for Him? What would He praise about your life and say, "Well done!" What areas do you think would grieve Him — what attitudes and actions would He want to work with you to change? Friend, surrender these latter things to Him in prayer and invite Him to bring transformation to these areas. It's your job to cooperate with the Holy Spirit — the Spirit Himself will bring the change.

Notes

Notes

Notes

CLAIM YOUR FREE RESOURCE!

As a way of introducing you further to the teaching ministry of Rick Renner, we would like to send you FREE of charge his teaching, "How To Receive a Miraculous Touch From God" on CD or USB format.

In His earthly ministry, Jesus commonly healed *all* who were sick of *all* their diseases. In this profound message, learn about the manifold dimensions of Christ's wisdom, goodness, power, and love toward all humanity who came to Him in faith with their needs.

☑ **YES, I want to receive Rick Renner's monthly teaching letter!**

Simply scan the QR code to claim this resource or go to: **renner.org/claim-your-free-offer**